Managing Editor
Ina Massler Levin, M.A.

Contributing Editor
Mara Ellen Guckian

Editor-in-Chief
Sharon Coan, M.S. Ed.

Illustrator
Blanca Apodaca

Cover Artist
Brenda DiAntonis

Art Coordinator
Kevin Barnes

Imaging
Ralph Olmedo, Jr.

Product Manager
Phil Garcia

Publishers
Rachelle Cracchiolo, M.S. Ed.
Mary Dupuy Smith, M.S. Ed.

Our Flag

Author

Polly Hoffman

Teacher Created Materials, Inc.
6421 Industry Way
Westminster, CA 92683
www.teachercreated.com
ISBN-0-7439-3596-9
©2002 Teacher Created Materials, Inc.
Made in U.S.A.

Teacher Created Materials

Table of Contents

Introduction

O'say does that star-spangled banner yet wave
O'er the land of the free and home of the brave!

As "The Star-Spangled Banner" is played, people all over the United States look upward to see our flag which has become the symbol of freedom throughout the world. *Our Flag* has been designed to give children the opportunity to find out more about this symbol of our nation. Students will find out how the American flag came to be and who helped it along the way.

In this unit full of activities for primary- and intermediate-aged children, there are several activities that connect to several areas of the curriculum including language arts, math, social studies, life skills, and music. These are not designed to be taught in any particular order but for the teacher to select activities that are appropriate for a particular class or group of students.

Our Flag offers patterns for bulletin boards, directions for student-created little books, puzzles, as well as a simple celebration that can serve as a culminating activity.

History and Background of Our Flag

When the Revolutionary War was fought from 1775–1783, the colonists fought under more than one flag. The first flag to represent all thirteen colonies was called the Continental Colors. It was also known as the Grand Union Flag. The British flag appeared in the top left corner of this flag. It served from 1775–1777 and was the first American flag to be saluted by another country.

When the Declaration of Independence was signed on July 4, 1776, it seemed inappropriate to include the British flag. It was then that the Continental Congress decided the new American flag would be red, white, and blue; have 13 stripes; and have 13 white stars on a blue field to represent the 13 original colonies. The red stripes are on the outside edges so that the flag can be seen against the sky. This new American flag received its first salute from another country on February 14, 1778.

It is not exactly clear who designed or made the first flag. Another delegate to the Continental Congress named Francis Hopkinson claimed he designed it. A gentleman by the name of William J. Canby claimed that his grandmother, Betsy Ross, made the first American flag. A seamstress in Philadelphia, Betsy Ross had made other flags during the Revolutionary War. She ran an upholstery business with her husband, John. After he died, she continued to run the business for several more years.

Canby claimed his grandmother had told him that General Washington had asked her to make the flag. He had suggested a design with 13 stars and 13 stripes, each star having six points. Betsy folded a piece of paper and made a five-point star approved of by General Washington. The 13 stars were placed in a circle with a blue background. She added the 13 alternating red and white stripes and the flag was adopted by the Continental Congress on June 14, 1777. Some historians found that the evidence in government records didn't prove what William Canby claimed. Although Betsy Ross may or may not have made the first American flag, it has been proven that she did make flags for the Pennsylvania state ships.

Over time, the flag has changed several times. The first flag had 13 stars to represent the 13 original colonies and 13 alternating red and white stripes. The next flag, in 1795, had 15 stars in rows for the 15 states along with 15 stripes. In 1818, the stripes were changed back to 13. There were 20 stars in five rows. It was decided that it was too cumbersome to keep adding stripes, as well as stars. Sometimes the 20 stars were arranged in the form of a star. In 1861, there were 34 stars, and from 1912–1959, there were 48 stars in rows.

History and Background of Our Flag *(cont.)*

In 1959, the flag was officially changed to 50 stars in alternating rows of six and seven, with the original 13 red and white stripes. This change was made to include Hawaii and Alaska, which joined the Union in 1959. The 50 star flag is what we celebrate today.

There are several national holidays when Americans display the flag proudly. June 14th is National Flag Day, and the flag is to be displayed. It also is displayed on Memorial Day, Independence Day, Labor Day, and Veterans Day, just to name a few. On Veterans Day and Memorial Day, the flag is to be displayed at half-staff until noon in honor of the soldiers who lost their lives. Veterans Day came about because World War I ended on the eleventh hour of the eleventh day of the eleventh month. It was originally known as "Armistice Day" to recognize the peace that was established that day. It became a national holiday in 1954 in hopes that people would strive for peace. There are often parades and celebrations on this day.

Because the flag is considered to be sacred, the Federal Flag Code was adopted on June 14, 1923, to maintain its integrity. The Federal Flag Code states guidelines for the treatment of the flag. It is very clear about things that should and shouldn't be done to the flag. The flag should never touch the ground and always be displayed on a pole, except for in extenuating circumstances like a funeral service for an American serviceman or dignitary. The flag should always be displayed outside of government offices, schools, and polling places. The flag should not be displayed when the weather is poor. When the flag is put away, there are specific guidelines as to how it should be folded. Traditionally, if the flag were to touch the ground, it was to be destroyed. The flag should always be displayed during the playing or singing of the National Anthem.

There is a great deal of history behind the American flag. Over the years it has had many names, including Old Glory, the Star-Spangled Banner, and the Red, White, and Blue. It says a lot about where and how the United States began, and where it is today. Most importantly, it represents the freedoms the citizens of the United States experience and live each day. The flag should be treated with great respect because of all it represents—the land, the people, and the government.

Betsy Ross

Betsy Ross was born in Philadelphia in 1752. She was a seamstress who shared an upholstery business in Philadelphia with her husband, John. When John was killed in an explosion in 1776, Betsy continued to run the business at the upholstery shop against the advice of her father.

Nearly 100 years later at a historical society meeting, Mrs. Ross' grandson, William J. Canby, first told what has become a famous story about his grandmother. He first remembered hearing the story when he was 11 and his grandmother was about 84 years old. He recollected that his grandmother told him that General George Washington asked her to make a flag for our country. General Washington suggested a design of 13 stars and 13 stripes. His stars had six points. Betsy made a beautiful five-pointed star by folding a piece of paper and making one snip. George was impressed. Five-pointed stars it would be! Betsy placed all 13 stars in a circle. The 13 stars and 13 stripes represented the 13 colonies existing at the time. The stars-and-stripes design was adopted by Congress on June 14, 1777.

For years and years, historians have searched government records and George Washington's writings in order to substantiate the information handed down within the Ross family. They have been unable to prove the legend. They have found, however, evidence to indicate that Betsy Ross did make flags for the Pennsylvania state ships.

Other descendants of Betsy Ross wrote the 1909 book, *The Evolution of the American Flag.* In the book, there is a picture of a painting showing Betsy Ross at a meeting of the committee of Congress. There are no records of this meeting. The artist, Charles H. Weisgerber, may have been speculating about what actually happened. The models he used were descendants of Betsy Ross. A flag with a circle of stars is shown in the painting. Photographs of that painting were later used in school textbooks, making any untruths difficult to dispel.

Many believe that there is no reason that Betsy, a Quaker, would have been making up stories about her life to tell her grandchildren. Quakers value modesty and truthfulness. More than one descendant remembers Betsy's stories, and the retellings are very consistent with each other.

During the war, there may not have been time to make clear records of every meeting that took place. However, one story tells of a fellow church member's visit to Betsy Ross' shop after her meeting with the Congressional Committee. The visitor saw the star that Betsy had cut for them, and he asked to keep it. In 1925, his family safe was opened to reveal that same star. It is now on exhibit at the Free Quaker Meeting House in Philadelphia.

Whatever the truth may be, most people enjoy the story of Betsy Ross and the making of the flag. As a result, it has become part of our history.

Flags of the U.S.A. Mini-book

Directions: Look at the different flags that have been official flags of the United States. Color the flag in each box. Cut out the boxes, place them in the correct order, and staple them in the top left corner to make a mini-book.

U.S. Flags Mini-Book

Name_____

The Continental Colors (1776) **1**

The first Stars and Stripes (1777) **2**

The 26-star flag (1795) **3**

The 30-star flag (1848) **4**

The 36-star flag (1864) **5**

The 48-star flag (1912) **6**

The 50-star flag (1959) **7**

The First Flag

The first United States flag had 13 stars and 13 stripes. Trace the stars. Color the flag.

1 = red	2 = white	3 = blue

Flag Math

Read the facts in the box. Solve the problems. Write the numbers in the boxes.

Our First Flag Facts

- It has 13 stars.
- There are 13 stripes altogether.
- There are 7 red stripes.
- There are 6 white stripes.

1. The number of stars minus the number of white stripes

 $-$ $=$

2. The number of red stripes plus the number of stars

 $+$ $=$

3. The number of stars minus the number of stripes altogether

 $-$ $=$

4. The number of white stripes plus the number of red stripes

 $+$ $=$

5. The number of red stripes minus the number of white stripes

$-$ $=$

The Flag and Betsy Ross

Background

Betsy Ross was born on January 1, 1752. She is credited with making what became the first flag of the United States. The flag she sewed together by hand in 1776 was adopted by the Continental Congress on June 14, 1777. Betsy Ross's original flag had 13 alternating red and white stripes and 13 white stars on a blue field. After a few changes in design when new states were added (at one point, there were 15 stars and 15 stripes), a law was passed in 1818 specifying that there would be 13 stripes to represent the 13 original colonies. A new star would be added to the blue field for each new state.

Making It Work

Give your students as much background about Betsy Ross as you think will interest them. Read the above paragraph to your students. Pages 4–6, and page 11 provide additional information. Use your classroom flag to demonstrate what you are describing when you point out the colors and the stars and stripes. Have reference books available, if appropriate.

Activity

You will need a classroom flag and a wall map of the United States. This activity is designed to be an oral exercise to establish a general base of information. See what the students already know and tell them the answers they don't know. Go back and repeat some of the questions and answers for reinforcement.

- Where did Betsy Ross live? Find it on a map. *(Philadelphia, Pennsylvania)*
- How did she sew the flag? *(by hand)*
- Why are the red stripes on the outside edges? *(so it can be seen against the sky)*
- What are some other names for the flag? *(Old Glory; the Star-Spangled Banner; the Red, White, and Blue)*
- How many stars did Betsy Ross's flag have? *(13)*
- How many stars does the flag have now? Why? *(50 stars, 50 states)*
- How many stripes did Betsy Ross's flag have? Why? *(13 stripes, 13 colonies)*
- How many stripes does the flag have now? Why? *(13 stripes, adding more would have made it an odd design or shape)*
- Which were the last two states to join the United States? When did they join? Find them on the map. *(Alaska, 49th, in 1959; Hawaii, 50th, in 1959)*
- What were the names of the 13 original colonies (states)? Find them on the map. *(Connecticut, Delaware, Georgia, Maryland, Massachusetts, New Hampshire, New Jersey, New York, North Carolina, Pennsylvania, Rhode Island, South Carolina, and Virginia)*

United States Flag

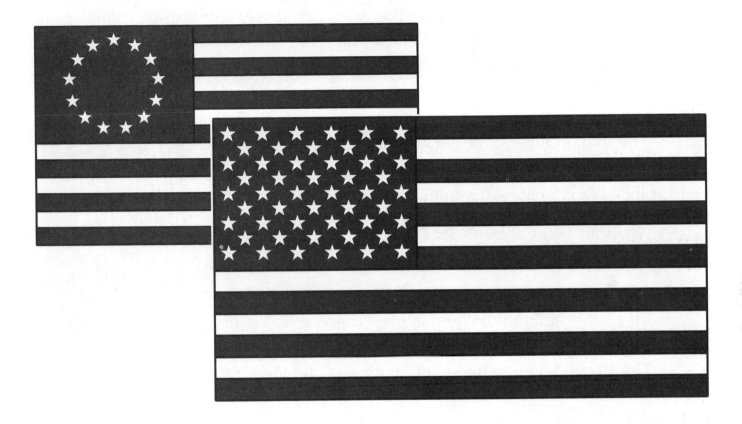

One of our most beloved national symbols is the American flag. It has changed many times over the years. The first American flag had 13 stars and 13 stripes to symbolize the original 13 colonies.

The colors chosen for the flag were important, too. The stripes alternated red and white, and the five-pointed stars lay on a blue background. Red symbolized valor or bravery, white stood for purity and goodness, and blue represented justice and fairness.

The plan was to add a stripe and a star each time a new state joined the union. It didn't take long for people to realize that if this plan were followed, the flag would quickly become much too large. Congress voted in 1818 to retain the 13 stripes in recognition of the original states and to add a star for every new state thereafter. Our flag now has 50 stars. Red, white, and blue are colors associated with America.

Find Out More on the Web

http://www.legion.org/flagtoc.htm—This site shows how to properly fold the flag and describes the symbolism involved in the flag-folding ceremony.

http://www.ushistory.org/betsy/flagstar.html—Visit the Betsy Ross Home Page and learn more about the flag. Find out how to cut a five-pointed star with just one snip of your scissors.

Displaying the Flag

Government offices and schools fly the flag every day. Many people display the flag on important national holidays: Presidents' Day, Independence Day, Memorial Day, Veteran's Day, and Flag Day (June 14).

The Federal Flag Code is a set of rules for displaying the flag. Here are some of those rules:

☆ The flag should not be flown outside in bad weather.

☆ The flag must never touch the ground.

☆ A flag should be flown near every school during school hours.

☆ No other flag may ever be placed above the U.S. flag.

☆ The flag may never be used in advertising of any kind.

☆ A flag in poor condition should be destroyed by burning.

☆ When the national anthem is played and a flag is displayed, all people should face the flag and salute.

☆ The flag is flown at half-staff to show mourning for the death of a high ranking government official or past president.

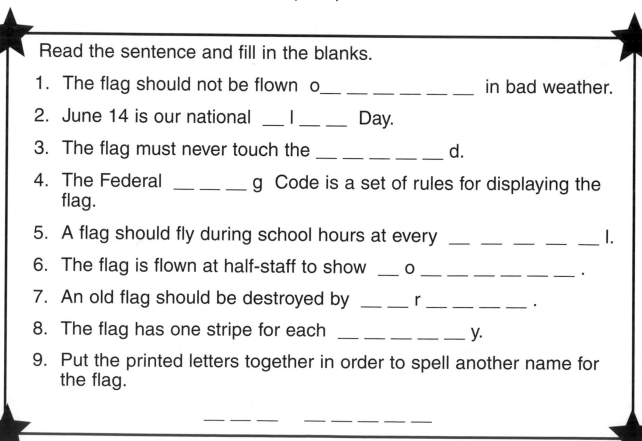

Read the sentence and fill in the blanks.

1. The flag should not be flown o__ __ __ __ __ __ in bad weather.

2. June 14 is our national __ l __ __ Day.

3. The flag must never touch the __ __ __ __ __ d.

4. The Federal __ __ __ g Code is a set of rules for displaying the flag.

5. A flag should fly during school hours at every __ __ __ __ __ l.

6. The flag is flown at half-staff to show __ o __ __ __ __ __ __ .

7. An old flag should be destroyed by __ __ r __ __ __ __ .

8. The flag has one stripe for each __ __ __ __ __ y.

9. Put the printed letters together in order to spell another name for the flag.

__ __ __   __ __ __ __ __

Folding the Flag

Here is how to correctly fold an American flag.

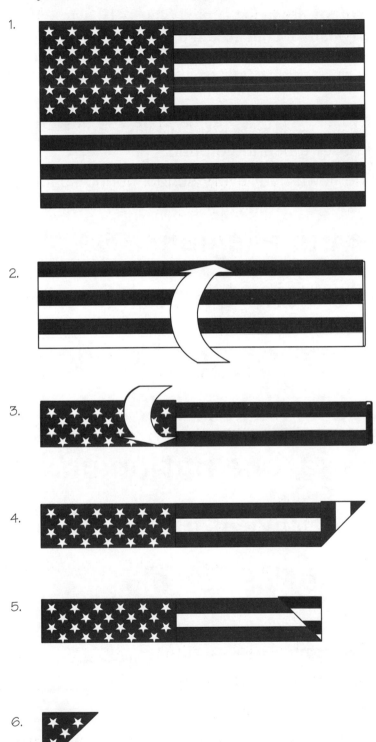

Practice: Turn a piece of paper into an American flag by coloring on it. Then, practice folding it like you would a real flag.

13

The Pledge of Allegiance

Francis Bellamy of Boston, Massachusetts, believed that American school children should make a promise of loyalty to the United States. He wrote the Pledge of Allegiance in 1892. Originally it contained the words, "my flag." Those words were changed in 1923 by the First National Flag Conference. In 1942, Congress made the pledge an official vow of loyalty to the United States. In 1954, the words "under God" were added.

Here is the Pledge of Allegiance as we say it today.

I pledge allegiance to the flag of the United States of America and to the republic for which it stands, one nation under God, indivisible, with liberty and justice for all.

Can you say the Pledge from memory? When you learn it, color the badge on page 16 and wear it proudly.

American Flag Cinquain

A *cinquain* is a five-line poem that contains the following lines:

Line 1—one word which names the subject (noun)
Line 2—two words which describe or define the subject (adjectives)
Line 3—three words that express action associated with the subject (verbs)
Line 4—a four-word phrase about the subject
Line 5—one word that sums up, restates, or supplies a synonym for the subject.

Brainstorm a list of words in the spaces below that describe the United States flag. When you have finished, choose the most appropriate words to create a cinquain about the flag.

Nouns	Adjectives	Verbs
_____	_____	_____
_____	_____	_____
_____	_____	_____
_____	_____	_____
_____	_____	_____

_____
(*subject*)

adjective _____   adjective _____
(*describing word*)   (*describing word*)

verb _____   verb _____   verb _____
(*action word*)   (*action word*)   (*action word*)

phrase _____ _____ _____ _____
(*four words about the subject*)

free line _____
(one-word summary or restatement)

Flag Rewards

I can say the first verse of

"The Star-Spangled Banner"

Congratulations to

_____

_____

_____   _____
Date   Teacher

is awarded this
GOOD CITIZEN
badge for

_____

Yes!
I can say the
Pledge . . .
Ask me.

"The Star-Spangled Banner"

In 1812, America again went to war against England. The English wanted America to stop trading with the French, and they were taking sailors from American ships. The British attacked the new capital, Washington, D.C., and burned the president's house and other buildings in 1814. When they went back to their ships, they took Dr. William Beanes as a prisoner.

President James Madison sent Francis Scott Key, a lawyer and a friend of Dr. Beanes, to Baltimore to get the British to release Dr. Beanes. Mr. Key convinced the British to free Dr. Beanes by proving that the doctor had cared for captured British soldiers with kindness and dignity. Although Francis Scott Key was successful in getting Dr. Beanes released, the two Americans were not allowed to return to Baltimore until after the planned battle. The British were about to attack Fort McHenry.

From the British ship, Francis Scott Key and Dr. Beanes watched the battle. It began at dawn on September 13th and continued through the night. The next morning, Francis Scott Key was so happy to see the American flag still flying that he wrote a poem, "The Defense of Fort McHenry," about how he felt. That poem was later set to music and called "The Star-Spangled Banner." Congress officially made "The Star-Spangled Banner" our national anthem in 1931.

Find Out More

Read *The Star-Spangled Banner* by Peter Spier (Bantam Doubleday Dell Books for Young Readers, 1992). This book contains the words and music for four verses of the song, as well as an illustrated evolution of the American flag from the time of the revolution.

"The Star-Spangled Banner" *(cont.)*

Answer these questions from the information you have just read on page 17.

1. Who burned the president's house in 1814? _____

2. Why did Mr. Key go to Baltimore? _____

   _____

3. From where did Mr. Key watch the bombardment? _____

4. What was the name of the poem Mr. Key wrote? _____

   _____

5. What is our national anthem? _____

   _____

6. When did Congress officially adopt the national anthem? _____

   _____

7. What do you think inspired Frances Scott Key to write this song? _____

   _____

8. What is a "star-spangled" banner? _____

   _____

9. Why do you think Mr. Key was happy when the flag was still waving the next morning? _____

   _____

10. How do you feel when you see the flag waving in the sky? _____

   _____

Singing the "Star-Spangled Banner"

Read and discuss these words of the American National Anthem. When you are done, try to sing it together as a class.

The Star-Spangled Banner

by Francis Scott Key

O say, can you see, by the dawn's early light,
What so proudly we hail'd at the twilight's last gleaming?
Whose broad stripes and bright stars, thro' the perilous fight
O'er the ramparts we watch'd, were so gallantly streaming?
And the rocket's red glare, the bombs bursting in air,
Gave proof thro' the night that our flag was still there.
O say, does that Star-Spangled Banner yet wave
O'er the land of the free and the home of the brave?

On the shore, dimly seen thro' the mists of the deep,
Where the foe's haughty host in dread silence reposes,
What is that which the breeze, o'er the towering steep,
As it fitfully blows, half conceals, half discloses?
Now it catches the gleam of the morning's first beam,
In full glory reflected now shines on the stream;
"Tis the Star-Spangled Banner, O long may it wave
O'er the land of the free and the home of the brave!

O thus be it ever when freemen shall stand
Between their loved homes and the war's desolation!
Blest with vict'ry and peace, may the heav'n rescued land
Praise the Pow'r that hath made and preserved us a nation!
Then conquer we must, when our cause it is just,
And this be our motto; "in God is our trust!"
And the Star-Spangled Banner in triumph shall wave
O'er the land of the free and the home of the brave!

19

Practicing Our National Anthem

The words to "The Star-Spangled Banner" were written in 1814 by Francis Scott Key as he watched the bombardment of Fort McHenry. They were set to the tune of an English drinking song. On March 3, 1931, President Herbert Hoover signed a bill that made the song the national anthem of the United States. Can you fill in the missing words in the first verse of "The Star-Spangled Banner"?

"O SAY, CAN YOU _____, BY THE _____ EARLY LIGHT,

WHAT SO PROUDLY WE _____, AT THE _____

LAST GLEAMING?

WHOSE BROAD _____ AND BRIGHT _____

THROUGH THE _____ FIGHT,

O'ER THE _____ WE WATCHED, WERE SO

GALLANTLY _____?

AND THE _____ RED GLARE, THE _____

BURSTING IN AIR,

GAVE _____ THROUGH THE NIGHT THAT

OUR _____ WAS STILL THERE.

O SAY DOES THAT _____ -SPANGLED BANNER YET WAVE

O'ER THE _____ OF THE FREE AND THE _____ OF

THE BRAVE?"

         #3596 Our Flag

National Anthem Puzzle Strips

Cut apart these strips. Mix them up and try to organize them in the correct order.

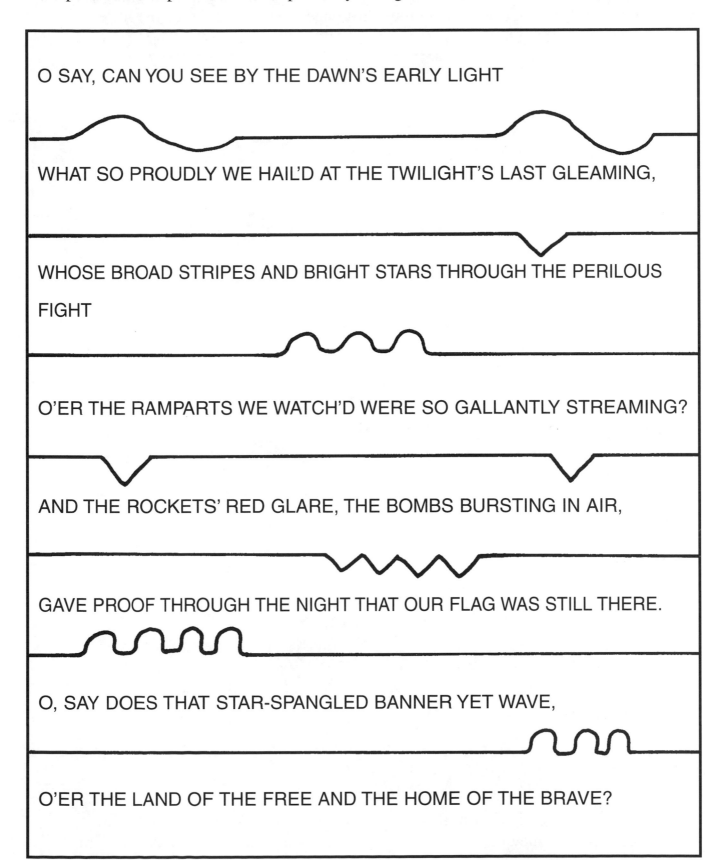

O SAY, CAN YOU SEE BY THE DAWN'S EARLY LIGHT

WHAT SO PROUDLY WE HAIL'D AT THE TWILIGHT'S LAST GLEAMING,

WHOSE BROAD STRIPES AND BRIGHT STARS THROUGH THE PERILOUS FIGHT

O'ER THE RAMPARTS WE WATCH'D WERE SO GALLANTLY STREAMING?

AND THE ROCKETS' RED GLARE, THE BOMBS BURSTING IN AIR,

GAVE PROOF THROUGH THE NIGHT THAT OUR FLAG WAS STILL THERE.

O, SAY DOES THAT STAR-SPANGLED BANNER YET WAVE,

O'ER THE LAND OF THE FREE AND THE HOME OF THE BRAVE?

National Anthem Little Book

Reproduce pages 22–24 for each child. Have them create a cover for the first page and draw a picture of the American flag on the last page. Have them color the little book and staple the pages together.

My National Anthem Book

_____

Name

During the War of 1812, the British had captured a prisoner named Dr. William Beanes. An attorney named Frances Scott Key was asked to try to rescue him. ①

National Anthem Little Book *(cont.)*

The British said they would not release Dr. Beanes, Mr. Key, or his companion until after they attacked Ft. McHenry.

②

Frances Scott Key watched from a ship in the early morning hours after the attack to see if the flag was still flying at the fort. When he saw the flag, he knew that America had won the battle. It inspired him to write what we know today as "The Star-Spangled Banner."

③

National Anthem Little Book *(cont.)*

O say, can you see, by the dawn's early light,

What so proudly we hail'd at the twilight's last gleaming?

Whose broad stripes and bright stars, thro' the perilous fight

O'er the ramparts we watch'd, were so gallantly streaming?

And the rocket's red glare, the bombs bursting in air,

Gave proof thro' the night that our flag was still there.

O say, does that Star-Spangled Banner yet wave,

O'er the land of the free and the home of the brave?

Our Flag

Patriotic Songs

Children love to sing songs. Below are patriotic words sung to familiar nursery rhymes. Use these songs throughout the day or to help get your students' attention in line. Use a book of sign language to help you add actions and the children can sing these songs at the culminating activity.

Flag, Flag, Beautiful Flag

(Sung to Baa, Baa, Black Sheep)

Flag, flag, beautiful flag,
How we love you,
Yes sir, yes sir,
All the days through.

First your beautiful stars,
Always shine through,
Then your thirteen stripes,
Red and white so true.

Flag, flag, beautiful flag,
How we love you,
Yes sir, yes sir,
All the days through.

Down by the Flag Pole

(Sung to Down by the Station)

Down by the flag pole,
Early in the morning,
See the students standing,
All in a row.

See the flag rising,
And waving too,
Red, white, and blue,
We salute you.

We Are Proud to Wave Our Flag

(Sung to Mary Had a Little Lamb)

We are proud to wave our flag,
Wave our flag, wave our flag.
We our proud to wave our flag,
And keep it flying high.

Uncle Sam

Who is that tall, bearded man wearing striped pants, a long tailcoat, and a tall hat covered with stars and stripes? It's Uncle Sam. There are several stories about how this figure become a symbol of the United States, but this is the one Congress officially recognized in 1961.

Samuel Wilson was born in Arlington, Massachusetts, in 1766. Later he moved to Troy, New York, and started a meatpacking business. During the War of 1812, Sam Wilson supplied meat to the United States Army in barrels marked "U.S." When asked what the initials stood for, one of Wilson's workers said they stood for the meatpacker, Uncle Sam Wilson. The story gained popularity when it was printed in a New York City newspaper. Soon many things labeled U.S. were being called Uncle Sam's.

Illustrators began to draw Uncle Sam as a symbol of the United States, using the same colors and stars-and-stripes designs as the American flag. In 1869, a famous cartoonist named Thomas Nast gave Uncle Sam a beard. During World War I, artist James Flagg used Uncle Sam on an army recruiting poster. On the poster, Uncle Sam points a finger at the person looking at him and says, "I Want You!"

Our Country's Flag

1. What three colors are on the United States flag?

   _____

2. What is the flag's nickname?

   _____

3. Who is said to have made the flag?

   _____

4. How many red stripes are there on the flag?_____

5. How many white stripes are there on the flag?_____

6. How many stars were on the first flag?_____

7. What does the red on the flag represent?

   _____

8. What do the stars on the flag represent?

   _____

9. For what purpose should the flag be flown at half-mast?

   _____

10. What does the white on the flag represent?

    _____

11. What does it mean when the flag is not flying at the White House?

    _____

12. When was the U.S. flag first flown on the moon? By whom?

    _____

13. How are the stars on the current U.S. flag arranged?

    _____

14. What does the blue on the flag represent?

    _____

15. Traditionally, if a flag touches the ground, what must be done with it?

    _____

U.S.A. Flag Math

Directions: If your teacher wishes, you may use a calculator to find the answers to the following mathematical problems.

1. The flag of the United States has five rows with six stars each and four rows with five stars each. How many stars are on the flag of the United States?

2. The Declaration of Independence was approved on July 4, 1776. It said that the United States was not any longer a part of Britain. How many years ago did the United States become free of Britain?

3. The United States made a law that the U.S. flag was to have 13 stars and 13 stripes for the 13 states. This law passed on June 14, 1777. Now June 14th is called Flag Day. How many years ago was the first Flag Day?

4. The first United States flag had 13 stars that stood for the original 13 colonies. How many more stars are on the United States flag now?

5. The Pledge of Allegiance was written by a man named Francis Bellamy in 1892. Congress made it a promise of loyalty to the United States in 1942. How long ago was it written?

6. The words for "The Star-Spangled Banner" were written as a poem by Francis Scott Key in 1814. He was happy because, even though the British were bombing Fort McHenry, in the morning the United States flag was still there. "The Star-Spangled Banner" became the national anthem in 1931 by an act of Congress. How many years after it was written did it become our national anthem?

1. _____   2. _____   3. _____   4. _____   5. _____   6. _____

Macaroni Sorting and Graphing

The flag is red, white, and blue. Give the children an opportunity to become very familiar with these colors while they work on their sorting and classifying skills. Have them sort the colored macaroni into groups then take that information and transfer it to paper by filling out the graph on page 30. Next, have them analyze the information gathered and share and compare it with their classmates.

Materials

- macaroni
- rubbing alcohol
- red and blue food coloring
- three large zipper plastic bags
- paper towel
- copy of page 30 for each child

Directions

1. Divide the macaroni into three equal parts. Put each part in a plastic bag.
2. In two of the bags, add one tablespoon of alcohol for every two cups of macaroni.
3. Add eight to ten drops of red coloring in one bag, and eight to ten drops of blue coloring in another bag. The third bag remains its natural color.
4. Close the bags and shake the bags well until the macaroni is colored. Add more food coloring if necessary.
5. Spread the macaroni out on the paper towel and let it dry for several hours before the students interact with it.
6. When dry, mix the colored and natural macaroni together.

Sorting and Graphing

1. Give each student a bag of colored macaroni and the graph on page 30.
2. Ask the students to sort and classify the macaroni. Then, record their results on the graph.
3. Discuss the results as a class.

Extension: When done sorting, graphing, and discussing the students' macaroni results, have them string the macaroni and beads or marshmallows on a piece of yarn or string to make a necklace. Ask them to make a pattern of red, white, and blue.

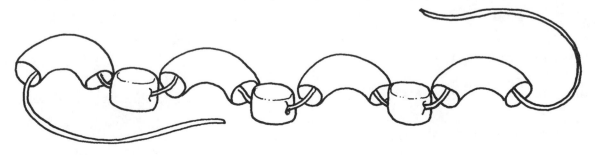

Macaroni Sorting and Graphing *(cont.)*

My Macaroni Graph

Red	**White**	**Blue**

The color I had the most of was _____.

The color I had the fewest of was _____.

As a class, we had the most_____.

Simple Flag Activities

The activities below are simple and require minimal preparation. These activities can be used as centers or with a small group of children.

Play Dough Flags

Give children red, white, and blue play dough during center time. Ask the children to make flags and other patriotic symbols. Let them dry and display them in the classroom.

Bakers Dough Flags

Use two parts flour, one part salt, and one part water to create a "bakers dough." Create small flags and place them on a cookie sheet. Bake at 350 degrees for about 20 minutes. Time may need to be adjusted as all ovens are different. Let cool completely. Use red, white, and blue craft paint to add color to your creations. Let them dry for 24 hours and then coat the flags with a clear spray paint for a finishing touch and to seal the paint.

Waving Flags

Have your students paint flags using water colors. There should be no part of the paper that isn't wet. If using white paper, paint the white stripes with water only. When finished painting the flag, sprinkle salt on top of the pictures and let them dry completely. The salt will make the colors run and blend, thus giving a waving flag effect. When dry, shake off the extra salt. Mount on another piece of red, white, or blue construction paper and display on the wall.

Torn-Paper Flags

Give each student one large piece of white construction paper and smaller pieces of red, white, and blue construction paper. Tell them to make a flag, but explain that they are not allowed to use scissors. They must tear very small pieces of paper and glue them on the large piece of white paper to represent the stripes, the blue background, and the stars. Display the flags in the hall or classroom accompanied with a patriotic saying.

Stars and Stripes Placemats

Give each student one large piece of red, white, or blue construction paper and several smaller pieces of red, white, and blue paper. Ask them to create a placemat to use at the flag celebration mentioned on the page 36. If possible, have the placemats laminated so they can be used over and over.

Puffy-Paint Flags

Combine equal parts of flour, salt, and water in a bowl. (Adjust the amount of ingredients depending on the number of students.) Mix well. Separate the mixture into three bowls. Add small amounts of tempera paint until the desired color is achieved. Pour the mixture into clean condiment containers. Old mustard containers work well. Have children draw patriotic pictures with the paint on heavy paper. Let the paint dry for 24 hours. Display the pictures in the classroom accompanied by a patriotic saying.

31

Patriotic Wind Sock

Make a patriotic wind sock using the materials and directions below. When you are done, hang your wind sock in the classroom or at home.

Materials:

- red and white crepe paper streamers
- blue construction paper, 9 x 18 inches (23 x 46 cm)
- glue, stapler, scissors, adhesive tape
- white chalk or silver glitter
- yarn or string

Directions:

1. Use the white chalk to make stars on one side of the blue paper. (If you wish, make the stars with silver glitter.)
2. Form the blue construction paper into a cylinder.
3. Glue closed along the shorter side. Staple to ensure stability.
4. Attach red and white streamers to one end with glue.
5. Cut three 12-inch (30.5 cm) lengths of string. Tape them about 6 inches (15 cm) apart to the top of the blue construction paper.
6. Knot the three strings together to make a hanger.

Patriotic Projects

Tissue Paper Flag

Make tissue paper flags with your students and use them on a bulletin board or send them home so your students will always have an American flag hanging in their house. It's important to help students realize that the American flag deserves tremendous respect, no matter what it is made of.

Materials

- one piece of 9" x 12" (22 cm x 30 cm) tag paper
- several pieces of red, white, and blue tissue paper
- plate or meat tray
- pencil
- ruler
- glue
- scissors

Making the Flag

1. Use the pencil to draw a flag on the piece of tag paper.
2. Cut the tissue paper into 1" (2.5 cm) squares.
3. Pour a small amount of glue on the plate.
4. Mold the small pieces of tissue paper around the eraser end of the pencil.
5. Dip the tissue paper into the glue and place it on the flag, removing the pencil in an upright position.
6. Place the red paper where the red stripes would be, white paper where the white stripes and stars would be, and blue around the stars.
7. Repeat the above process until the flag is completely covered with tissue paper.

Option: Use the template on page 8. Delete the numbers and make copies on tag paper. Ask the students to cover it with the tissue paper, following the directions above.

Patriotic Projects *(cont.)*

Hand-Painted Flag

The activity below is wonderful for cooperative learning. Divide the children into groups of four or five students. Give them the materials they will need and tell them they must plan their flag very carefully. They must decide the exact measurements, who is going to make handprints, and in what color. They may decide everyone makes handprints, and they may decide to keep one person clean to help with organization. This would also be a great activity to use with buddies in an older grade level. Giving children the opportunity to work and plan together helps them learn the value of compromising.

Materials

- white or tan butcher paper, 5' long (4.5 m)
- red, white, and blue paint
- pencil

Making the Hand-Painted Flag

1. Lay the butcher paper flat on the ground and, using the pencil, lightly draw the basic parts of the flag. Double check that there are 13 stripes and 50 stars before you begin painting.

2. Dip your student's hand in the red paint and place his or her hand on an appropriate stripe. Continue this process until all the red stripes are covered with paint.

3. If using white paper, leave the space open where the white stripes would be. If not, repeat the process using white paint on the other stripes.

4. Paint the entire square blue where the stars would be.

5. Have your students make white thumb prints on the dry, blue background, to represent stars.

6. Hang the finished flag on the wall. Create a border of red, white, and blue stars.

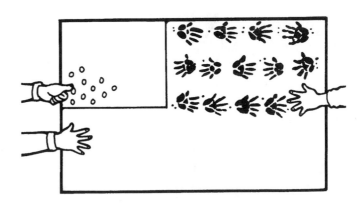

Extensions

★ Make the flag big enough to cover an entire wall by using several pieces of butcher paper cut to the right proportions.

★ Have students dictate patriotic sayings and type them on the computer. (Flying high for freedom, The flag was still there!, The red, white, and blue forever true. etc.) Staple the sayings randomly on the flag after it is hung.

Patriotic Projects *(cont.)*

Patriotic Stepping Stone

Make a stepping stone and keep it in a school garden. This activity works well with a small group of students.

Materials

- heavy duty tape
- cement mix
- stir stick
- trowel or flat tool
- several red, white, and blue tiles
- small or medium pizza box
- large bucket
- water
- very sharp pencil
- hammer

Directions

1. Prepare the tiles by breaking them into small pieces. (Use a hammer, if necessary.)
2. Mix the cement according to the directions.
3. Reinforce the corners of the pizza box with tape and fill it with cement, leaving about ½" (2 cm) at the top.
4. Smooth the cement with a trowel and let it stand for 15 minutes.
5. Use a pencil and the tiles to decorate the stepping stone.
6. Let it dry for 24–48 hours before moving the tile or removing it from the box.

Flag Celebration

Have a celebration when your study of the flag is complete. First, decorate the classroom and gather red, white, and blue party supplies. Next, decide on the foods you will serve. Have students brainstorm a list of foods that are the colors of the flag. For instance:

red—watermelon, strawberries, cherry pie, cherry gelatin, strawberry jam, spaghetti sauce, etc.

white—vanilla ice cream, white cake and white frosting, coconut, white bread without the crusts, pasta, etc.

blue—blue gelatin, blueberries, etc.

Students could also try the recipes below.

Star-Spangled Punch

- 64 oz. container of raspberry/cranberry juice
- 2-liter container of lemon lime soda
- small container of frozen raspberries
- small container of fresh blueberries

Combine the above ingredients in a large punch bowl or pitcher. Serve each cup of punch with a few berries in it and enjoy.

Graham Cracker Flags

Ingredients

- one large graham cracker
- white frosting
- three 6" (15 cm) pieces of red string licorice
- four 3" (8 cm) pieces of red string licorice
- blue food coloring
- small zipper snack bag
- scissors
- craft stick or dull knife

Directions

1. Using the craft stick, spread white frosting on the entire graham cracker.
2. Use the blue food coloring and a small amount of the white frosting to make blue frosting. Spread blue frosting on the top left corner, one half across and half way down the graham cracker.
3. Place the three 6" (1.5 cm) pieces of licorice on the bottom half of the cracker to represent the longer stripes, and the four 3" (8 cm) pieces on the top right half of the cracker, next to the blue frosting, to represent the four shorter stripes.
4. Put a small amount of white frosting in the zipper bag and use the scissors to cut off the very tip of the bag. Use the bag of frosting like a cake decorator would and make as many white stars, or dots, in the blue square as you can.

The Colors of the Flag

The United States flag is *red*, *white*, and *blue*. *Red* represents bravery, *white* represents purity, and *blue* represents justice. There are 50 white stars in the upper left corner that represent the 50 states in America. Each star points to the top of the flag. There are 13 stripes on the flag that represent the 13 original colonies. Red stripes are on the outside to make the flag more visible when flying.

A lot of thought went into designing the flag and the colors. Each color was chosen for a specific reason. When countries or organizations design a flag to represent them, they choose certain colors because of what they represent.

Design a Class Flag

With the help of the color key below, design a flag to represent your class. When finished, write a short paragraph describing why you chose the colors you did and what they represent.

Homework: Family Flag

Send paper, the color key, and other materials that might be needed home with the students. Ask them to sit down with their family, and using the color key, design a family flag. Have the children share their completed flags with the class. Display the flags on a bulletin board with the saying: *Each of our families is unique and special in its own way.*

Color Key

blue = justice, piety, sincerity	**black** = grief, sorrow
green = hope	**orange** = strength, endurance
purple = high rank	**red** = courage, valor
red-purple = sacrifice	**silver** or **white** = faith, purity
yellow or **gold** = honor, loyalty	

37

Fill in the Blanks

Use this activity to double check what your students have learned about the American flag. This can be used for review before a test or culminating activity.

Betsy Ross	**Francis Hopkinson**	**seven**
bravery	**ground**	**six**
Continental Congress	**half-staff**	**stars**
dawn	**July 4, 1776**	**stripes**
Declaration	**justice**	**the government**
dusk	**left**	**the land**
folded	**purity**	**the people**

Directions: Use the words in the box to fill in the blanks in the sentences below.

1. The _____ of Independence was signed on _____.

2. On June 14, 1777, the _____ decided the flag would have 13 stripes.

3. A delegate to the Continental Congress by the name of _____ _____ claimed he designed the flag.

4. It is said that _____ sewed the first flag.

5. The flag has _____ red stripes and _____ white stripes.

6. The red in the flag stands for _____.

7. The white in the flag stands for _____.

8. The blue in the flag stands for _____.

9. The _____ and _____ is the most popular name for the United States flag.

10. The Stars and Stripes stand for _____, _____, and _____.

11. The flag should be displayed between _____ and _____.

12. Never let the flag touch the _____ .

13. The stars should be on the upper _____ side.

14. When the flag isn't being used, it should be carefully _____ .

15. After a tragic event, the flag is often displayed at _____ .

I Know About the Flag

39

Crossword Puzzle

Use this crossword puzzle as a review of what the children have learned about the American flag. Use the words below to complete the sentences and fill in the puzzle.

American
flag
fold
July
nation
Old Glory
Pledge
pole
Ross
six
stars
stripes
U. S. A.

Across

3. The _____ is red, white, and blue.
4. There is a specific way to _____ the flag.
6. School children sometimes say the _____ of Allegiance before school.
7. It is said that Betsy _____ made the first flag.
10. There are thirteen _____ on the flag.
11. There are ____ white stripes on the flag.
13. The abbreviation for the United States of America is _____.

Down

1. The United States is a free _____.
2. The flag often hangs on a _____.
5. Another name for the flag is _____ _____.
8. There are fifty _____ on the flag.
9. Citizens might say that they are proud to be _____.
12. We celebrate our independence on the 4th of _____.

Flag Word Search

Directions

Find the words related to the flag in the word bank. The words may appear across, up, down, backwards, or diagonally in the diagram. Find each word and circle it, keeping in mind that some letters may appear in more than one word.

Word Bank

Betsy Ross	Flag	Nation	Stars
Citizen	Honor	Patriotic	Stripes
Continental	Independence	Pledge	U. S. A.
Declaration	July	Seven	Veteran
Display	Loyal	Six	Washington D. C.

Bonus Words: American Freedom

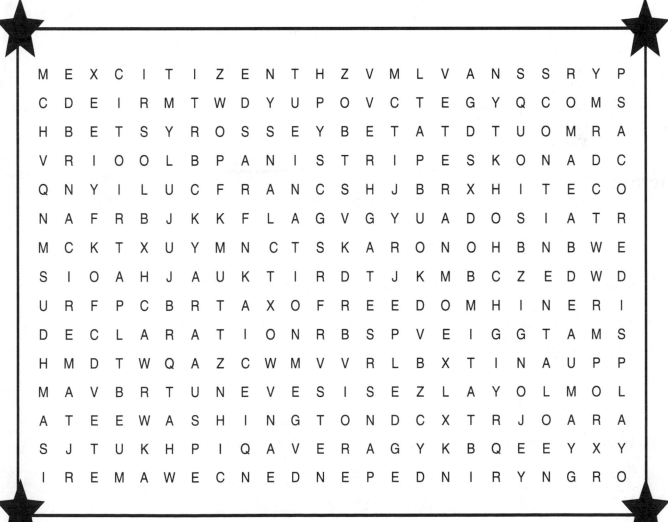

```
M E X C I T I Z E N T H Z V M L V A N S S R Y P
C D E I R M T W D Y U P O V C T E G Y Q C O M S
H B E T S Y R O S S E Y B E T A T D T U O M R A
V R I O O L B P A N I S T R I P E S K O N A D C
Q N Y I L U C F R A N C S H J B R X H I T E C O
N A F R B J K K F L A G V G Y U A D O S I A T R
M C K T X U Y M N C T S K A R O N O H B N B W E
S I O A H J A U K T I R D T J K M B C Z E D W D
U R F P C B R T A X O F R E E D O M H I N E R I
D E C L A R A T I O N R B S P V E I G G T A M S
H M D T W Q A Z C W M V V R L B X T I N A U P P
M A V B R T U N E V E S I S E Z L A Y O L M O L
A T E E W A S H I N G T O N D C X T R J O A R A
S J T U K H P I Q A V E R A G Y K B Q E E Y X Y
I R E M A W E C N E D N E P E D N I R Y N G R O
```

Displaying the Flag

Directions: There are specific guidelines for saying the Pledge of Allegiance and displaying the flag. Read the paragraphs below and answer the questions that follow.

Although we have many freedoms in the United States, we are still expected to be respectful when it comes to saying the Pledge of Allegiance and displaying the flag. When a person says the Pledge of Allegiance, he or she is to be standing, facing the flag, with his or her right hand over his or her heart. If wearing a hat, it should be removed with the right hand and placed over the heart. People in uniform should salute the flag.

There are many guidelines to follow when displaying the United States flag. The Federal Flag Code was passed to protect the integrity of the flag. The flag should be displayed from sunrise to sunset, and properly folded when taken down. A flag may be displayed 24 hours a day if properly illuminated at night. If the weather is poor, the flag should not be displayed. When in a parade or marching situation, the flag should always be on a staff and be on the right if with one other flag, in front and center if there is a line of flags. On election days, the flag should be displayed in front of every polling place. It should also be displayed in front of or near every institution of learning, like a school. If using a flag on a vehicle, the flag should be firmly attached to the chassis or attached to the right fender. When the flag is flown with city or state flags, particularly when sharing a staff, the United States flag should always be hoisted first, or on top. When flags of two or more nations are flown, they should be on separate staffs. The flag should always be flown at half-staff after a national tragic event. Often times, it is flown at half-staff after the death of a firefighter or a police officer. Out of respect, it is a general rule that the flag should never touch the ground.

1. How should one position his/her body when saying the Pledge of Allegiance?

2. What should one do with a hat when saying the Pledge of Allegiance?

3. People in uniform should do what when saying the Pledge of Allegiance?

4. From what time to what time should the flag be displayed, and what is the exception to the rule?

5. What should happen to a flag when taken down?

6. In a parade situation, how should the flag be displayed?

7. There should always be a flag displayed in front of what?

8. How should a flag be displayed with flags of other nations?

9. After a tragic event, how should the flag be displayed?

10. Why should a flag never touch the ground?

Bulletin Board Ideas

A Flag of Hands

One way to introduce the American flag to the other students is by using a bulletin board in the school. Use the idea from page 34, making a large flag with paint and handprints. Start out by measuring the amount of paper needed to cover an entire section of a wall, in the classroom or hallway. You may need to borrow a ladder or step stool in order to reach the higher parts of the flag. Be sure to have an adult on each side of the ladder or step stool to ensure the students' safety. Frame the flag with a student-made border. Measure the length of each side and cut strips of white adding machine tape to the correct length. Ask each student to write a patriotic saying, then decorate their section of the tape. Hang the now decorated tape around the flag.

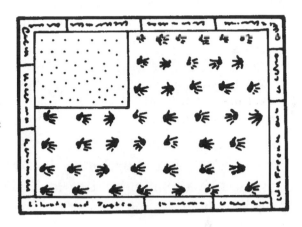

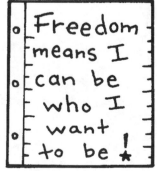

Tissue Paper Flags

Use the idea from page 33 to create this bulletin board. Each student makes a tissue paper flag. Mount the flag on another colored piece of construction paper so that two sides look like they are framed. Then, ask your students to write what freedom means to them. Primary students will enjoy writing something to share with other students. If working with intermediate-age children, limit the length of the paper to ten sentences or less and use wide-lined paper. Other children around the school are more likely to stop and read something that is in large print. Again, frame the flag with a student-made border.

Veterans Day

Veterans Day is a day that honors those men and women who have served their country in the United States Armed Forces. November 11th is the day these special people are honored.

In our country, Veterans Day was not always known by that name. On November 11th, 1918 (the 11th hour of the 11th day of the 11th month), World War I ended. This was known as "The War to End All Wars" and people all over the world rejoiced. The day became known as "Armistice Day" in honor of the truce of peace that was made on this day.

Armistice Day became a day to recognize those people who had fought so courageously in World War I and to celebrate the peace that now existed. November 11th was designated as a federal holiday in 1938. But shortly after this holiday was declared, World War II broke out. The dream of "The War to End All Wars" was now gone. Many lives were lost during this second world war, and those who lost loved ones and those who fought for their country needed to be recognized as well as those World War I patriots.

In 1954, Congress changed the name of Armistice Day to Veterans Day in order to honor United States veterans of all wars. At this time, President Eisenhower asked all Americans to strive for peace.

In the United States, people remember the men and women who fought for freedom on Veterans Day with ceremonial flag raisings, celebrations, parades, speeches, and special services. It is a day to honor all the veterans who have served our country.

United States Marine Corps
War Memorial

Independence Day

On Independence Day, the Fourth of July, the people of the United States celebrate the anniversary of the founding of our democratic nation. The signs of the holiday are everywhere. Flags are unfurled around the countryside, people cover the parks and recreation areas with picnics, Uncle Sam leads town parades, patriotic music fills the air, and spectacular fireworks light up the sky! It is a noisy, joyous day!

Independence Day is the birthday of the United States. On July 4, 1776, over 200 years ago, the United Colonies of America adopted the document which declared the United States to be "Free and Independent States," and that "all political connection between them and the State of Great Britain, is and ought to be totally dissolved." This document was the Declaration of Independence which gave all who lived in these new United States the equal right to "Life, Liberty, and the Pursuit of Happiness."

The Declaration of Independence set up the foundation for freedom and democracy in our country and inspired many people throughout the world to be free.

The first Independence Day celebration took place in Philadelphia on July 4, 1777. It was a grand day of festivity. Through the years, the Fourth of July has been kept as a special holiday by the people of the United States. It's a day filled with historic remembering, a rededication to democracy, and a whole lot of fun!

Flag Word Bank

This Word Bank is a handy reference tool for creative writing, vocabulary development, social studies, and more.

flag pole	nation	Stars and Stripes
Fourth of July	National Anthem	stripes
Francis Scott Key	Old Glory	tradition
free	President	unfurl
freedom	red	Union
George Washington	sewing	United States of America
honor	Star-Spangled Banner	wave
Independence	stars	white

Betsy Ross	Congress
billow	British
blue	ceremony
brave	colonies
	Continental
dusk	
fabric	
five-point	

Bibliography

Primary

Bateman, Theresa O'Brien. *Red, White, Blue and Uncle Who?* Holiday House. September, 2000.

Bates, Katherine Lee. *America the Beautiful.* Atheneum. September, 1993.

Bellamy, Francis. *The Pledge of Allegiance.* Scholastic. May, 2001.

Binns, Triston Boyer. *The American Flag (Symbols of Freedom).* Heineman Library. 2001.

D'Aulaire, Ingri. *The Star Spangled Banner.* Applewood Books. November, 2000.

Herman, John. *Red, White, and Blue: The Story of the American Flag.* Grosset and Dunlap. April, 1998.

Kroll, Steven. *By the Dawns Early Light.* Scholastic. July, 2000.

Penner, Lucille Recht. *The Statue of Liberty (Step into Reading Step 1).* Random House. July, 1995.

Ryan, Pam Munoz. *The Flag We Love.* Charlesbridge Publishing. July, 2001.

Wallner, Alexandra. *Betsy Ross.* Holiday House. 1994.

Intermediate

Quiri, Patricia Ryon. *The American Flag (True Books, American Symbols).* Children's Press. 1998.

Spencer, Eve. *A Flag for Our Country (Stories of America).* Raintree/Steck-Vaughn. May, 1996.

Weil, Ann. *Betsy Ross.* Aladdin Paperbacks. October, 1996.

West, Delno and Jean M. West. *Uncle Sam and Old Glory.* Atheneum. February, 2000.

Whipple, Wayne. *The Story of the American Flag.* Applewood Books. July, 2001.

Websites

www.timepage.org
The history behind the American flag and the ratifying of the flag by the original thirteen colonies

www.ushistory.org/betsy/flagtale.html
The American tale of Betsy Ross

www.learn2.com/09/0903/0903.html
Step-by-step instructions for folding the American flag

www.sar.org/colors/flag.htm
Flag history and etiquette

www.usflag.org
History behind the flag and lyrics to patriotic songs

www.Americanhistory.si.edu/ssb/
Exhibit from National Museum of American History and the story of the flag

Answer Key

Page 9
1. 7
2. 7, 13, 20
3. 13, 13, 0
4. 6, 7, 13
5. 7, 6, 1

Page 12
1. outside
2. Flag
3. ground
4. Flag
5. school
6. mourning
7. burning
8. colony
9. Old Glory

Page 18
1. the British
2. to rescue Dr. Beanes
3. the ship
4. "The Defense of Fort McHenry"
5. "The Star-Spangled Banner"
6. 1931
7–10. answers will vary

Page 27
1. red, white, blue
2. Old Glory or Stars & Stripes
3. Betsy Ross
4. 7
5. 6
6. 13
7. bravery
8. the states
9. in a tragic event
10. purity
11. The president is not home.
12. 1969, Neil Armstrong, Buzz Aldrin
13. in alternating rows—five rows with six stars each and four rows with five stars each
14. justice
15. destroyed

Page 28
1. 50
2. answers may vary
3. answers may vary
4. 37
5. answers may vary
6. 117 years

Page 38
1. Declaration, July, 4,1776
2. Continental Congress
3. Francis Hopkinson
4. Betsy Ross
5. seven, six
6. bravery
7. purity
8. justice
9. Stars, Stripes
10. the land, the people, the government
11. dawn, dusk
12. ground
13. left
14. folded
15. half-staff

Page 40

Across
3. flag
4. fold
6. Pledge
7. Ross
10. stripes
11. six
13. U.S.A.

Down
1. nation
2. pole
5. Old Glory
8. stars
9. American
12. July

Page 42
1. standing, facing the flag, with right hand over heart
2. remove hat
3. salute
4. dusk and dawn, except when illuminated at night
5. folded properly
6. flag should be on a staff
7. in front of every polling place and every school
8. Each nation should have its own staff.
9. half-staff
10. out of respect

Page 41

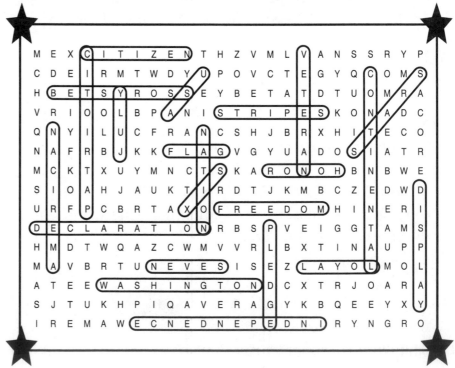